Toxic Creatures

# The Blue-Ringed Octopus

Laura L. Sullivan

Cavendish Square
New York

Published in 2018 by Cavendish Square Publishing, LLC
243 5th Avenue, Suite 136, New York, NY 10016



First Edition



Library of Congress Cataloging-in-Publication Data

Names: Sullivan, Laura L., 1974- , author.
Title: Blue-ringed octopus / Laura L. Sullivan.
Description: New York : Cavendish Square Publishing, 2017. | Series: Toxic creatures | Includes index.
Identifiers: LCCN 2016052782 (print) | LCCN 2016054774 (ebook) | ISBN 9781502625984 (pbk.) | ISBN 9781502625809 (6 pack) | ISBN 9781502625946 (library bound) | ISBN 9781502625854 (E-book)
Subjects: LCSH: Blue-ringed octopuses--Juvenile literature.
Classification: LCC QL430.3.O2 S887 2017 (print) | LCC QL430.3.O2 (ebook) | DDC 594/.56--dc23
LC record available at https://lccn.loc.gov/2016052782

Editorial Director: David McNamara
Editor: Fletcher Doyle
Copy Editor: Nathan Heidelberger
Associate Art Director: Amy Greenan
Designer: Alan Sliwinski
Production Coordinator: Karol Szymczuk
Photo Research: J8 Media

The photographs in this book are used by permission and through the courtesy of: Cover, p. 1 YUSRAN ABDUL RAHMAN/Shutterstock.com; throughout book, Deliverance/Shutterstock.com; p. 4 kaschibo/Shutterstock.com; p. 6 Jens Petersen/Wikimedia Commons/Hapalochlaena lunulata2.jpg/CC BY-SA 3.0; p. 7 Andrew J Martinez/Science Source/Getty Images; p. 8 Chris Newbert/Minden Pictures/Getty Images; p. 9 Auscape/Universal Images Group/Getty Images; p. 11 Puwadol Jaturawutthichai/Shutterstock.com; p. 12 DEA/FOTO THELMA & LOUISE/De Agostini Editorial/Getty Images; p. 14 Steve Childs/Flickr.com/CC BY 2.0; p. 15 Geoff Brightling/Dorling Kindersley/Getty Images; p. 16 David Jones/PA Images/Alamy Images; p. 17 Jurgen Freund/Nature Picture Library/Getty Images; p. 18 dsi/iStock/Thinkstock; p. 19 decade3d/Shutterstock.com; p. 21 Ron Dahlquist/Perspectives/Getty Images; p. 22 nimon/Shutterstock.com; p. 24 vm/E+/Getty Images; p. 25 eggeegg/Shutterstock.com; p. 26 Ethan Daniels/Stocktrek Images/Getty Images.

Printed in the United States of America

# CONTENTS


1 Small Wonder ........ 5

Blue-Ringed Octopus Quick Facts ........ 10

2 Double Danger ........ 13

3 Home in Danger ........ 23

Toxic Creatures Quiz ........ 28

Glossary ........ 29

Find Out More ........ 30

Index ........ 31

About the Author ........ 32

The blue-ringed octopus is very small, and very deadly.

CHAPTER ONE

# Small Wonder

The blue-ringed octopus is tiny, but its venom is deadly. Blue-ringed octopuses are invertebrates, which means they have no backbone. They have soft, flexible bodies. They can squeeze into very small places. Their eight arms have many suction cups, which they use to grasp prey. At the center of the arms is a parrot-like beak.

Blue-ringed octopuses live in tide pools and on shallow **reefs**. They are small and soft. Some sharks

*Like other octopuses, the blue-ringed octopus is a master of camouflage, even with the rings showing.*

and eels will eat them. Blue-ringed octopuses spend most of their lives hiding. They come out only to eat or find a mate. They can change the color of their skin. Then they can blend in with their environment.

## Warning Signal

Most of the time, their blue rings are not visible. Their blue rings flash a warning signal when they sense danger. Most other octopuses can squirt out a jet of ink to confuse **predators**. The blue-ringed octopus has no ink. It relies on its toxin to protect it when it isn't hiding.

*When this octopus is calm, its rings are much less visible.*

Blue-ringed octopuses eat lots of shrimp and crabs. Sometimes they eat fish. They have good vision. This lets them see prey at night. They can swim between 5 and 10 miles per hour (8 to 16 kilometers per hour). They grasp their prey in their arms, using the suction cups to hold them. Then they bite with their strong beaks, injecting venom. This **paralyzes** their prey.

*When a blue-ringed octopus bites, its prey is soon paralyzed. This one is eating a crab.*

*Blue-ringed octopus mothers guard their eggs until they hatch.*

## Starving for the Babies

The blue-ringed octopus reproduces just once. The male dies a few weeks after mating. The female will lay up to fifty eggs in a safe place such as a crevice, a large empty shell, or even in a glass bottle. She will guard the eggs until they hatch several months later. She doesn't eat for the entire time. The babies are the size of a pea when born. After the eggs hatch, the mother octopus dies.

## Blue-Ringed Octopus Quick Facts

**Name:** Blue-ringed octopuses get their common name from the blue rings that decorate their bodies. Their genus name, *Hapalochlaena*, means "soft skinned." The greater blue-ringed octopus is *Hapalochlaena lunulata*. Lunulata means "little moons."

**Range:** The blue-ringed octopus is found in the Pacific and Indian Oceans. They are most common off the coast of Australia.

**Size:** All species are small. The largest, the southern blue-ringed octopus, is about 8 inches (20 centimeters) from the top of its head to the tips of its arms. The smallest, the blue-lined octopus, reaches only about 2 inches (5 cm) long. The greater blue-ringed octopus is between those two lengths. It is named for the large size of its rings, not its body size.

**Species:** There are at least three species of blue-ringed octopuses: the greater blue-ringed octopus, the southern blue-ringed octopus, and the blue-lined octopus. A fourth species is known from just two specimens. Other species are still being investigated.

**Fun Fact:** Octopuses are the most intelligent invertebrates. They can use tools and solve puzzles. Captive octopuses often break out of their tanks and explore.

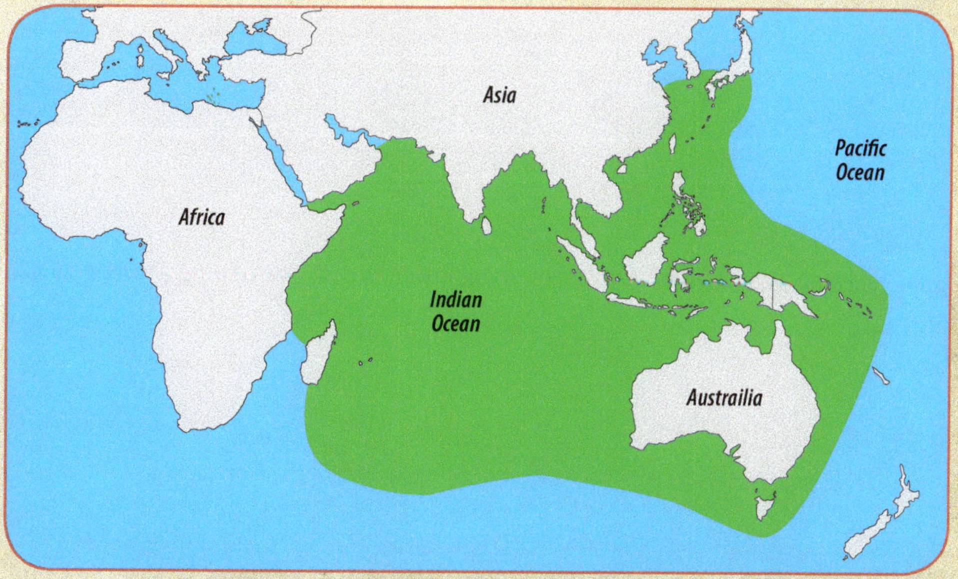


*The blue-ringed octopus is found in the Pacific and Indian Oceans (marked in green).*

The blue-ringed octopus bites with its beak, and toxic saliva enters the wound.

CHAPTER TWO

# Double Danger

Many living things make toxins, which they use to defend themselves. A toxin is a harmful substance made by an animal, plant, fungus, or other living creature. A toxin is a poison if it causes harm by being swallowed or absorbed through the skin. A toxin is a venom if it causes harm by being injected with a fang, barb, or spine. The blue-ringed octopus is unusual. It is both venomous and poisonous.

All octopuses are venomous, but only blue-ringed octopuses have venom that can hurt humans. The venom is in their **saliva**. They have two large salivary glands that produce two kinds of venom. One is effective against their prey but has no effect on humans. The other venom, called **tetrodotoxin**, is extremely dangerous to humans. When the octopus

*Although blue-ringed octopuses are deadly, some people pick them up because they are small and pretty.*

*The venom, called tetradotoxin, is found in the salivary glands, shown here in orange.*

bites with its parrot-like beak, the toxic saliva enters the wound. There is enough venom in one blue-ringed octopus to kill about ten people.

## Helpful Bacteria

Tetrodotoxin is found in several other poisonous and venomous animals. Among them are puffer fish, moon snails, and rough-skinned newts. The animals don't make the toxin. It is made by a **bacteria** that lives inside of them. These bacteria live in the blue-ringed octopus's salivary glands. They have a **mutualistic** relationship. They help each other, like honeybees and flowers. The octopus provides the bacteria with a good place to live. The bacteria give the octopus the toxin for defense.

Tetrodotoxin is found in other parts of the blue-ringed octopus. If a person ate a blue-ringed

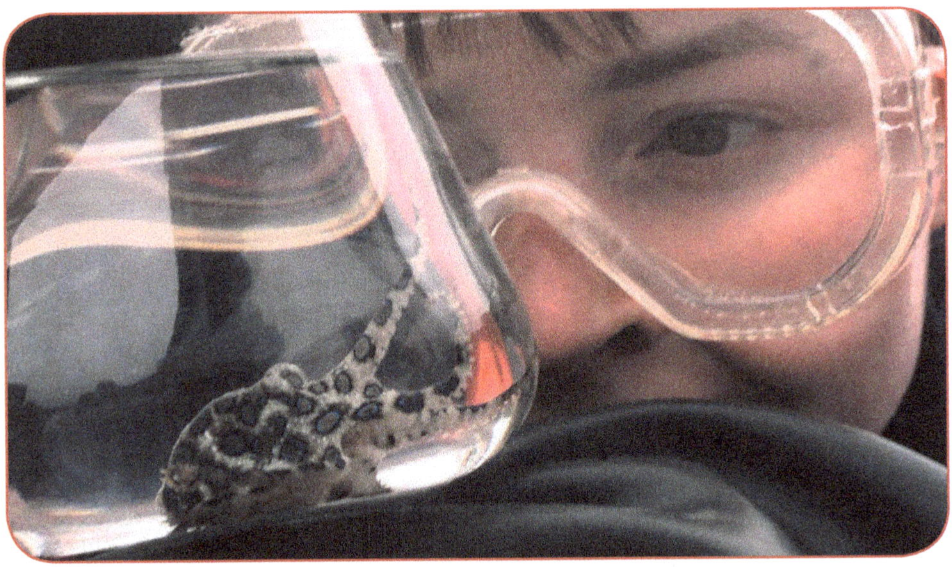

*Some blue-ringed octopuses are very tiny, but they still have enough venom to kill several people.*

octopus, the toxin would still be harmful. This is not true of many other venomous animals, such as a rattlesnake. If a person swallowed rattlesnake venom, the stomach acids would destroy it, and the person would not be harmed. However, tetrodotoxin is not destroyed by stomach acid. If a person swallowed it, he or she would get very sick or die. Blue-ringed octopuses even release toxin into the water. Someone who touched a blue-ringed octopus, or

*If the octopus can't hide, it will usually try to swim away.*

stuck his or her hand in the tank of a captive one, might get a numb hand or other symptoms. Blue-ringed octopuses are poisonous and venomous because the toxin works when injected, eaten, or absorbed.

Blue-ringed octopuses are not aggressive. They prefer to flee or hide when threatened. Bites are rare.

*Some Australian beaches have warning signs about the dangerous blue-ringed octopus.*

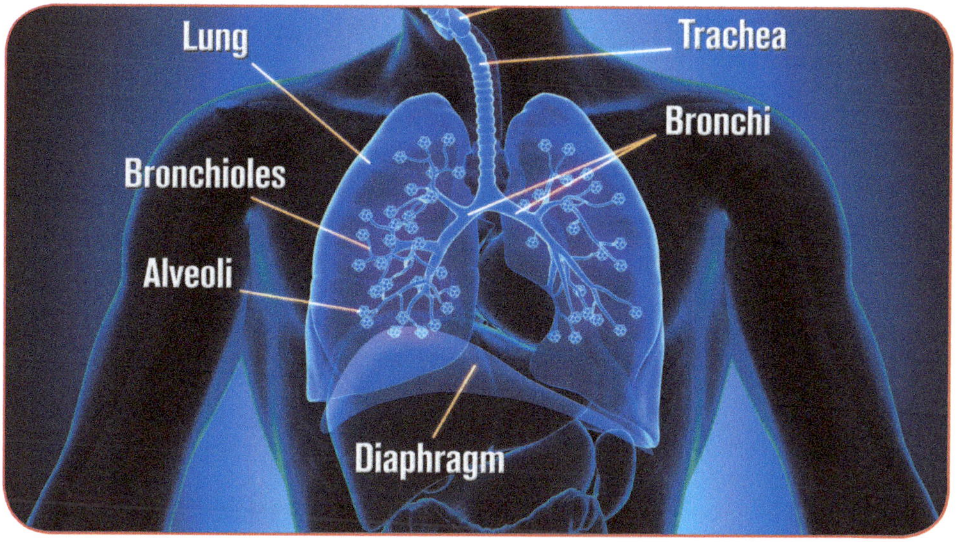


*The diaphragm—the muscle that controls breathing—is paralyzed by blue-ringed octopus venom.*

They usually happen if someone accidentally steps on an octopus or reaches into a hole without looking. Some people think blue-ringed octopuses are cute and pick them up.

## Fast-Acting Venom

Victims say that the bite is almost painless. However, within minutes, severe symptoms begin. They start with numbness and tingling. Nausea, vomiting, and blurred vision follow. Soon, muscles become weak. Tetrodotoxin stops nerves from sending signals to the body's voluntary muscles. Before long, the **diaphragm**—the muscle that controls breathing—is paralyzed. The victim can no longer breathe. The heart will keep beating until the victim runs out of oxygen. The brain is unaffected. A victim will be aware of what is happening until he or she runs out of air.

There is no antidote or antivenom to tetrodotoxin. The only treatment is to keep the victim breathing through **artificial respiration**. As long as rescue breathing is continued, the victim will probably survive. It takes several hours for the toxin to leave the body. Without artificial respiration, a victim will die after a few minutes, when the brain stops getting oxygen.

## Deadly Discovery

The blue-ringed octopus was given its scientific name by **mollusk** specialist Guy Coburn Robson in 1929. Before that, though, the indigenous people of Australia almost certainly knew it was toxic. The first recorded death in Australia from a blue-ringed octopus bite was in 1954, when a spear fisher was killed.

*Spear fishers and curious swimmers are at risk of being bitten.*

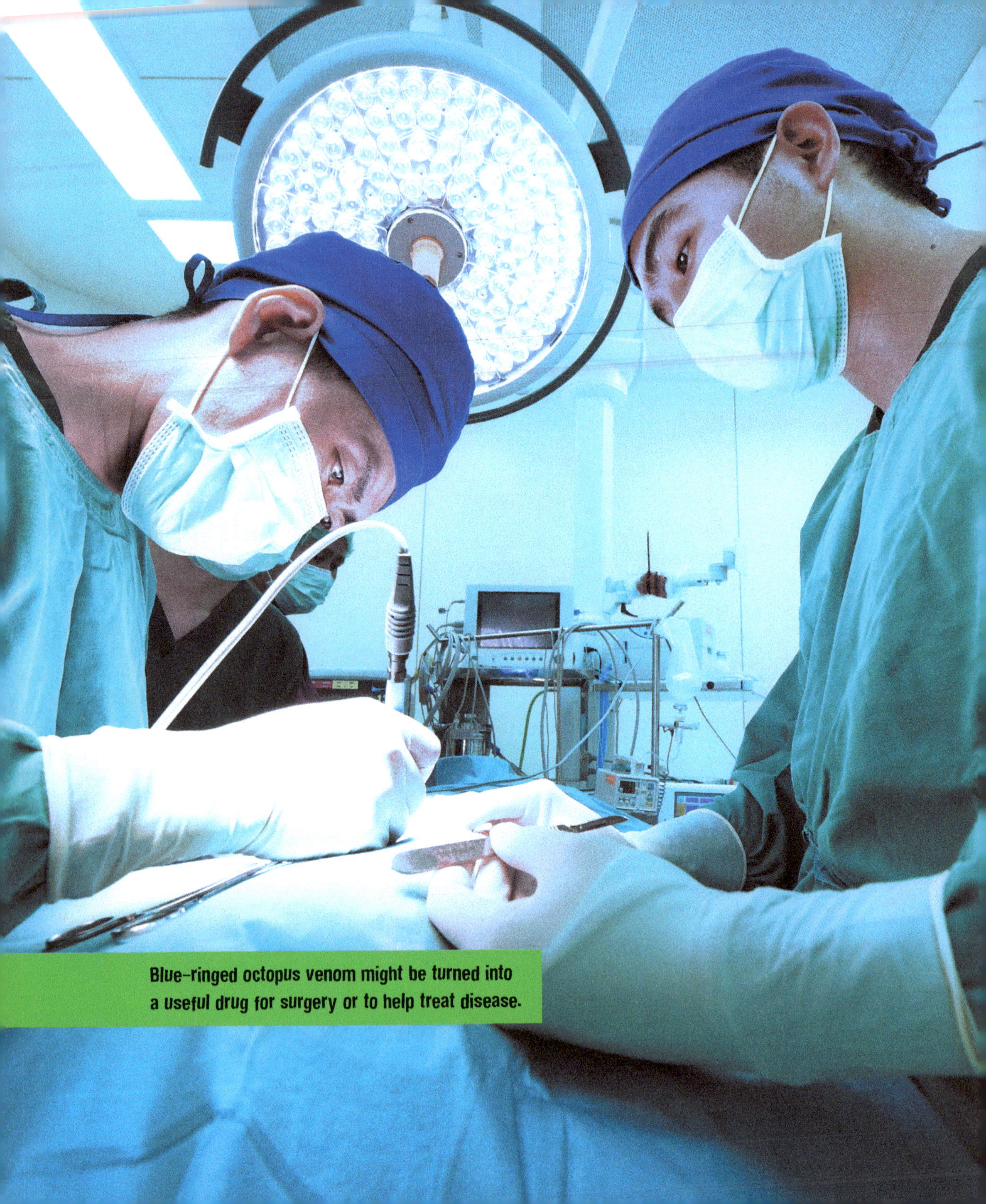

Blue-ringed octopus venom might be turned into a useful drug for surgery or to help treat disease.

CHAPTER THREE

# Home in Danger

The difference between a medicine and a poison can be the dose. Toxins produced by animals can be valuable sources of drugs that can help people. At high doses or in natural toxic form, toxins can produce things like paralysis, which is deadly. However, paralysis can be useful. During some surgeries, patients must not move. Even if they are unconscious, they might need a drug that stops

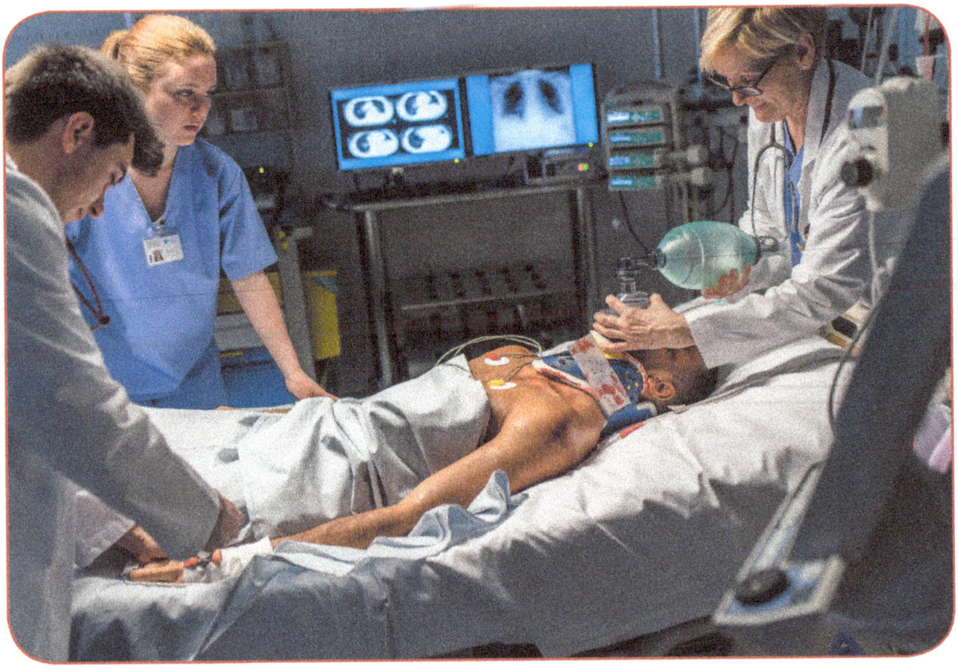

*The same venom that might put a victim in the hospital could one day help other patients survive.*

involuntary movements. Blue-ringed octopus toxin is among several toxins being tested for this use.

Tetrodotoxin causes a loss of sensation. The toxin is being tested as a painkiller for people suffering from extreme pain due to cancer. Other scientists are looking at tetrodotoxin to treat bad headaches called migraines.

*Blue-ringed octopus toxin might one day help migraine sufferers.*

## Reefs Threatened

Despite its deadly potential, the blue-ringed octopus is a valuable part of its environment. And its habitat—coral reefs around Australia—is under serious threat. The Great Barrier Reef is the largest coral reef in the world. It is being destroyed by

*The blue-ringed octopus's environment is being destroyed by several factors, including coral bleaching.*

several things. Fertilizer runoff causes algae blooms that can kill marine life. Pesticides, overfishing, and an invasion of crown-of-thorns starfish, which prey on corals, also threaten the Great Barrier Reef.

The biggest threat is climate change. Warming waters cause coral bleaching, a condition that weakens, or even kills, corals. It can also keep coral from reproducing fast enough to survive. Since 1985, the Great Barrier Reef has lost about half of its coral. If this continues, the blue-ringed octopus and many other marine creatures could become extinct.

## Toxic Creatures Quiz

1. Are a blue-ringed octopus's blue rings clearly visible at all times?
2. Explain how a blue-ringed octopus is both venomous and poisonous.
3. Why are blue-ringed octopus bites uncommon?
4. What things threaten the blue-ringed octopus's home, the Great Barrier Reef?

### Answer Key

1. No. When the octopus is calm, the rings are faint and brown. When the octopus is alarmed, though, the rings flash blue in warning.
2. The toxin can be injected with saliva when the octopus bites (venomous), and it is also harmful if it is eaten or absorbed through the skin (poisonous).
3. Blue-ringed octopuses are very shy and prefer to hide or flee from people.
4. Pollution, fertilizer, overfishing, crown-of-thorns starfish, and climate change.

# GLOSSARY

**artificial respiration** Putting air into the lungs of a person who can't breathe on his or her own.

**bacteria** A group of one-celled organisms, some of which are useful, others of which can cause disease.

**diaphragm** The muscle between the chest and the abdomen that helps with breathing.

**mollusk** A group of invertebrates that includes clams, snails, slugs, and octopuses.

**mutualistic** A beneficial relationship between two species.

**paralyze** To cause to be unable to move.

**predator** An animal that hunts other animals for food.

**reef** A system of rocks or coral near the surface of the water.

**saliva** Liquid released into the mouth by glands; it helps with chewing and digesting food.

**tetrodotoxin** A toxin that can cause paralysis and death.

# FIND OUT MORE

## Books

Montgomery, Sy. *The Octopus Scientists*. New York: HMH Books for Young Readers, 2015.

Olsen, Alana. *Look Out for the Blue-Ringed Octopus*. Surprisingly Scary. New York: PowerKids Press, 2015.

## Websites

**Aquarium of the Pacific: Blue Ringed Octopus**

http://www.aquariumofpacific.org/onlinelearningcenter/species/greater_blue_ringed_octopus1

This site from California's Aquarium of the Pacific has a lot of detailed information on the blue-ringed octopus, including details about its feeding habits.

**National Geographic Kids: Octopus**

http://kids.nationalgeographic.com/animals/octopus/#octopus.jpg

Learn all about the many kinds of octopuses in this site from National Geographic. It includes links to articles about octopus intelligence.

# INDEX

Page numbers in **boldface** are illustrations. Entries in **boldface** are glossary terms.

algae blooms, 26
**artificial respiration**, 20
Australia, 10, **11**, **18**, 21, 25
**bacteria**, 16
beak, 5, 8, **12**, 15
climate change, 27
coral bleaching, **26**, 27
**diaphragm**, **19**, 20
eggs, 9, **9**
Great Barrier Reef, 25–27
ink, 7
invertebrates, 5, 11
medicine, 23–24
**mollusk**, 21
**mutualistic**, 16
**paralyze**, 8, 20, 23–24
**predator**, 7
**reef**, 5, 25–27
Robson, Guy Coburn, 21
**saliva**, 14–15
salivary glands, 14, **15**, 16
species, 10–11
suction cups, 5, 8, **12**
symptoms, 18–20, 23–24
**tetrodotoxin**, 14–17, 20, 24
treatment, 20
venom, 5, 8, 13–15, 17

## ABOUT THE AUTHOR

**Laura L. Sullivan** is the author of more than forty fiction and nonfiction books for children, including the fantasies *Under the Green Hill* and *Guardian of the Green Hill*. She has written many books for Cavendish Square, including four titles in the Toxic Creatures series.